AF538564

Yes I Can

Other books by Author

Yes I Can

Sumer Sethi, MD

Published by
PRABHAT PRAKASHAN PVT. LTD.
4/19 Asaf Ali Road,
New Delhi-110 002 (INDIA)
e-mail: prabhatbooks@gmail.com

ISBN 978-93-90923-27-4
YES I CAN
by Dr. Sumer Sethi

Edition
2025

Illustrations
Ms. Shashi Gupta

Price
₹ 250.00 (Rupees Two Hundred Fifty only)

Printed at
R-Tech Offset Printers, Delhi

Contents

Foreword

I am honoured and delighted to write the foreword of the book *Yes I Can* by Dr. Sumer Sethi not only because he has been my husband, a friend and colleague for more than ten years, but because I also like him deeply believe in that a positive attitude is the key for long-lasting change and which will encourage you to think positively and provide you with a daily dose of energy. Two of the most positive thoughts one can have are, Yes I Can deal with it and second I'll always find my way no matter what happens. These two thoughts take you to believe in yourself and think positively about the future. So would you like to believe in yourself? Then this book is for you as it helps you to build a strong positive attitude so that you can determine the course of your life and achieve your goals and dreams with ease. This simple book, *Yes I Can*, on positive attitude is a perfect way to develop an attitude that is simply contagious and influences others and is a great option for anyone in search of not only an overview of positive attitude but actionable steps one can take in their lives. It motivates you to succeed and inspires you to greater heights to find happiness in everyday things. Thinking positively is to always believe in success and not to believe in defeat because most obstacles are mental in character. You will discover in this book how you can find your purpose, a purpose that gives meaning to your life, a purpose that helps you live your life to the fullest, a purpose that allows you to see yourself and most things in a positive light.

If there is something in this world that can teach you how to be more positive, that something is this book. Would you like to think more positively about yourself? Then read this book and become the master of your thoughts and self-beliefs. Many people tell you just believe in yourself, and you can do it but not too many understand what that actually means or how to put it in practice. Whatever makes you say, I can't help it, I can't do or I can't change it, makes you become a slave to human conditioning. Being a slave to self-defeating thoughts can kill your self discipline, lower your self-esteem, and ultimately doubt yourself at every step you make.

The book narrates you how to learn to be more optimistic, think positively, and become the best version of you. By believing in yourself you can face no matter what life put in front of you.

Believing in yourself makes almost everything else rosy and easy. Is it not?

Because of that fact, what you believe about yourself becomes a reality. If you say you can, your unconscious mind does its best to prove you are right. This magnificent book helps you to build your positive self-belief to take charge of your life, not to fear commitment, value your word and honour above feeling free to do whatever you want.

Yes I Can is challenging the way you think about yourself and how you see and think about the future, motivates and inspires you to march forward with confidence and get the things you want out of life. The book might be what you were waiting for to get inspired and progress even further. The knowledge in this book can be your perfect ground on which to build self-discipline; small steps, after small steps until you're at the top of the Mountain. So in brief we can say that positive attitude is a skill that one can learn. Make that learning enjoyable and comfortable by reading this book *Yes I Can*.

—Dr. Deepti Sethi

Acknowledgements

My Parents Dr. Subhash Chander Sethi and Mrs. Karuna Sethi for being a constant source of encouragement and inspiration throughout.

My wife Dr. Deepti Sethi for her support and patience without which this project would never have been possible. My son Krish for bearing with me in the manuscript preparation. Your support is my backbone.

Thanking you for blessings and support Mr. Deepak Bahl and Mrs. Geeta Bahl.

Dr. Sidharth Kumar Sethi, Dr. Shilpa Singla, Ms. Sumati, Mr. Sameer Bahl and Ms. Adity Bahl for the wishes and support. Dr. Rajiv Bhagi for all his support always.

Mr. Aayush Sharma for his immense contribution in getting everything organized meticulously and always believing in the possibility of this book.

Ms. Shashi Gupta for her artwork and illustrations which has made this book complete.

Prologue

He was home for a short trip. And just when he planned to go back to the city, he heard the news of the entire country under lockdown because of some mystery illness spreading out from China. He could not go back to the city. He was stuck. Day after day, there was no news of the train services resuming. However, experiencing the lockdown life, he realised the importance of social interaction.

He began to miss the ordinary realities of the pre-lockdown world and struggled with the loneliness and feeling of isolation.

Having plenty of time for himself has led him down the unending road of introspection. He began to realise the flaws in the life he lived.

Bored of doing nothing, one fine evening as he was walking along the street in his home town, he spotted his school teacher SS Sir. Yes, he was the

one. Seemed older and more frail, but definitely he was the one. He had a boundless passion for teaching and learning. A real teacher, talented, bright, and all around cool guy...he explored everything. He was a great listener and he impressed upon him the importance of reaching for knowledge. He truly delighted in teaching and learning.

Funny he had never thought of the school all these years.

He had no idea, how things would change.

He never expected his world, his entire thinking process and his approach to life would change after meeting SS Sir.

He approached him and touched his feet as is customary in Indian town to give respect to teachers. SS Sir didn't recognise him for some moments and then gave a smile of recognition. It was so good to see him. There were so many memories from school. He was always the bright student from school and SS Sir's favourite. SS Sir would always smile at him and encourage him. He used to tell sir, that one day, he will become someone special. Those were the days. Now, in city, he was working in an ordinary office. Nothing special. All those promises of school brilliance meant nothing. He was a no body in a big city. While strolling, they started remembering old times and other teachers. Many of the teachers had left school and one of his favourites biology teacher had recently retired. SS Sir had a wrinkled but handsome face. His eyes were bright and smiling. Yes, they were always like this, even in those years. May be the eyes don't age, he thought. In between somehow, in the conversation, he started telling him about his disappointing job and what a failure he has been. All that promise, all that potential that his school teachers saw in him, never really came through. SS Sir looked at him with concern. Sir had to go back. So he had invited him for a cup of tea at his residence, which he had accepted. When SS Sir was walking down the lane, he noticed Sir had aged and there was certain slowness in his walk. But the grace and calm were still the same as olden days.

This book is a narrative of the conversation he had with Sir on that day and many more days in that month, as the lockdown continued. For the sake of the flow and clarity, here onwards this book will be from his perspective.

Yes
I
Can

1

Yes I Can

The whole day I kept waiting for the cup of tea with my favourite teacher SS Sir as I knew that a cup of tea shared with such a visionary person would be happiness tasted and time well spent. Living in a big city far from your family is not that easy. You might not have the time to share your regrets, fallacies and pain and where is the scope for your dreams, journeys and imaginations. Thinking this cup of tea would give me an excuse to be with my favourite teacher, to listen to some of his visions and to share some of mine. With these thoughts I reached at his residence and found him waiting for me. He greeted me and introduced me to other members of his family. I tried to make myself comfortable but my mind was racing.

I couldn't wait and wanted to ask him

something, but words were losing me. I wanted to ask him why my life was so miserable. Why the promise I showed in the school never really happened in the real life. But, still stayed silent. Finally, after a few minutes I asked, Sir, what is it that you saw in me when I was your student that made you believe in me. He looked at me, with his thoughtful eyes, for a moment. I was sure his mind at that moment was processing years of memories of students like me or he might not remember anything about me. After few moments he started speaking. His these words changed my approach towards life here onwards. He said, you were the kid who always said yes to every challenge his teachers and his peer group could think of. Yes, that was correct, as a kid I used to participate in all school activities with great enthusiasm. Always interested to try new things, wanting to take on challenges

He said, you were the kid who always said yes to every challenge his teachers and his peer group could think of. Yes, that was correct, as a kid I used to participate in all school activities with great enthusiasm.

and would never say no to any task, challenge or any activity. Then I wondered, that is not me nowadays. I have become of more of grumbler nowadays, always complaining about everything. Going to office in the morning and coming back in the evening has become my monotonous routine and I have never shown any interest in any new challenge. But then, at least I have a job. Suddenly his voice, interrupted my chain of thoughts. He asked me do you know the power of Yes. I looked perplexed; he went on to explain. Just like he always did in those mesmerizing classes in school days. I still remembered how he used his hands and body language to explain things. In his class you always had to be attentive as he could ask questions anytime to anyone.

"Let me share an idea which helps me a lot and I believe it will help you to find ways and solutions to your problems. I will call it, the attitude of Yes, I can. Do you know what leaders do when they are stuck with a difficult situation? They look for solutions. Imagine yourself in your office and you are in a leading position. Let's assume because of this lockdown scenario, your office and work flow are in a bad shape. What would you do? What I saw in you was a youngster who would try to solve; who would take responsibility in such a situation and say—Yes, I Can. Someone must take charge and take responsibility. Someone must make it happen. In my team, I always try to be the solution finder. I try my best to find a way. Because I believe, whatever problem we are facing today or we are suffering or we are having an issue today, there are solutions to those problems somewhere. And sometimes it works, sometimes it doesn't. But whenever it works, the respect that the team has for me grows because they know that I'm working hard to solve the problem. This is what they call an attitude of Yes, I Can. Yes, I Can means that I have a response to the problem. Anybody who puts a problem to me, as they say, let's try to solve it. But do not take it as arrogance. I don't know everything that is truth. And I accept it in front of my students and with my team members. It's OK not to know at times. So Yes, I Can is not an attitude of

What I saw in you was a youngster who would try to solve; who would take responsibility in such a situation and say—Yes, I Can. Someone must take charge and take responsibility.

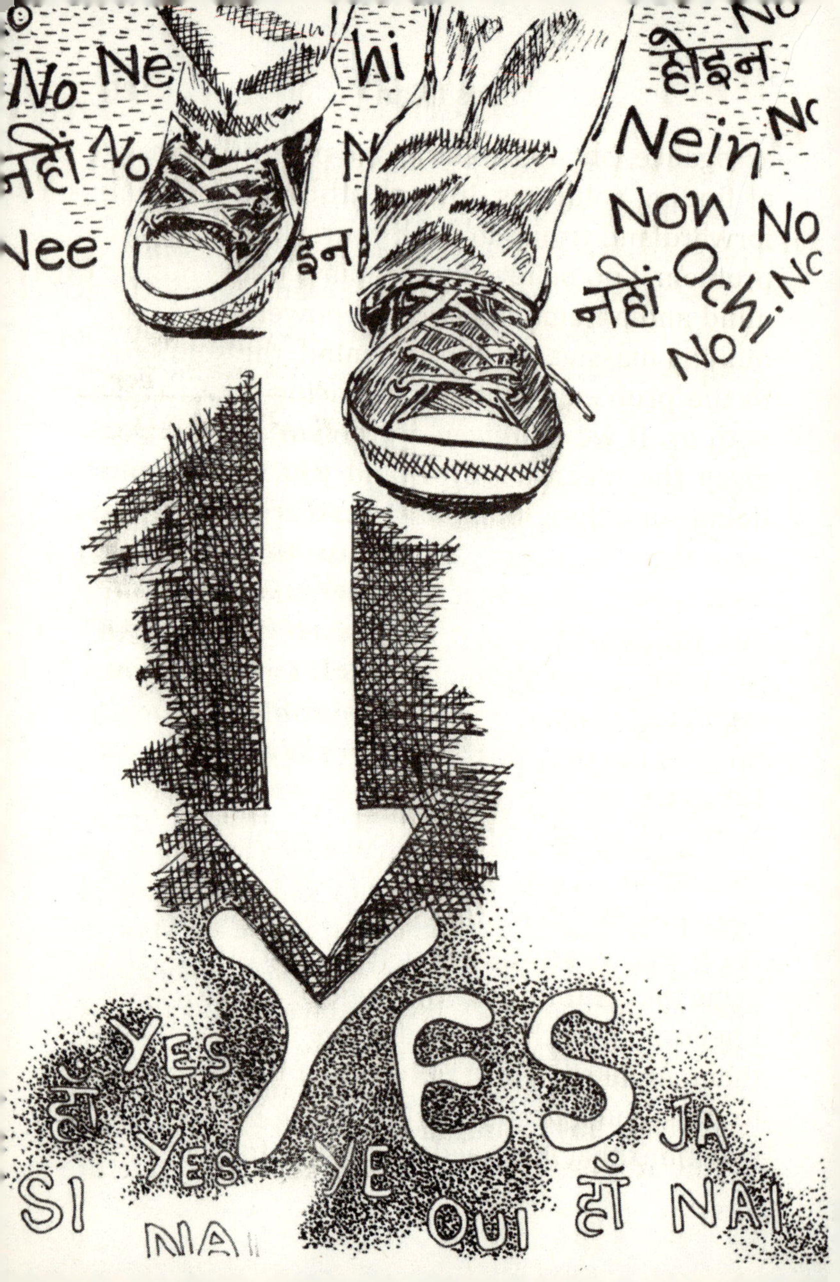
No
Ne
hi
होइन
नहीं
No
Nein
Nee
इन
Non
No
नहीं
Ochi
No
YES
YES
हाँ
YES
JA
SI
NA
OUI
हाँ
NAI

arrogance, but Yes, I Can is the positive attitude of finding solutions. It is an attitude of moving forward and trying to push yourself to solve the problem. I do believe in the ability of the human mind and a human being. The power of a single mind is massive. It is in our mind, the solutions to the problems that we are facing are already with us. If we are given a problem, we are also given the means. Why would you think about doing something great as a child, if you did not have the capability? So you have the capability. That is something that you need to understand, and you need to say it to yourself; you need to say it in case of problems. Yes, I Can. Once you say it, Yes, I Can, it is your responsibility to work, to work the best possible to get to the answers. Let us try to solve it.

To all my students, I keep telling them that let's try to be a problem solver. Let's not be the people who are finding problems. I always tell them that if you bring a problem to me, also bring the solution. As I want you to say, Yes, I Can. I believe these three words have great power in them. And I want you to tell me if this helps you to solve some problems that you're facing, some questions that you needed answers to.

All this while I was nodding my head, I knew the reason, might be I was not taking the challenges that my career was throwing at me. Might be that is what changed in me from my school time. I was no longer saying—Yes. Might be I needed to be back to schooldays and remembering my mentors to learn these three words—Yes, I Can. Then I realised that I am the captain of my destiny. I have the power to change. The power to improve. My thoughts were interrupted by his gentle hand on my shoulder. I touched his feet and asked, if I could come again tomorrow; he said sure. He always enjoyed the company of his students. For him I was still his student and may be I needed him more than ever before.

Might be that is what changed in me from my school time. I was no longer saying—Yes. Might be I needed to be back to schooldays and remembering my mentors to learn these three words—Yes, I Can. Then I realised that I am the captain of my destiny.

□

2

The Default 'Yes'

Next day, I was ready to go to his residence in the evening with the feeling that my SS Sir might be able to revive the same enthusiastic, promising student that I was during my school days. Yes, his words of the previous day had given me a hope and also shown me some direction. But still I was having few questions in my mind which I wanted to ask him. At the same time, I also felt that Sir might be trying to oversimplify the things. He is not understanding that life in a school is very different from the complex life in an office in a metropolitan city where one cannot say Yes at times. It might work for him in a small town but what about in a corporate world.

I reached his place and found him waiting for me. He greeted me with a smile. After few minutes of a general talk, I asked him, what did he mean by always saying yes to the problems. He looked at me and started speaking:

"I will tell you about a small incident which happened few months back. Many students and their parents would come to me to discuss and seek advice regarding the performance of their children in competitive exams. Now, this is about one such student whose parents came to me to discuss about career trajectory of their child. While talking to them, I came to know that this student was one of the top scorers of our school, but was not doing well in competitive exams and his parents wanted me to help him in the upcoming exam. I asked the child about his performance in the recent exam and found that he had not given the exam. According to him he was not very well prepared for that particular

Many students and their parents would come to me to discuss and seek advice regarding the performance of their children in competitive exams. Now, this is about one such student whose parents came to me to discuss about career trajectory of their child.

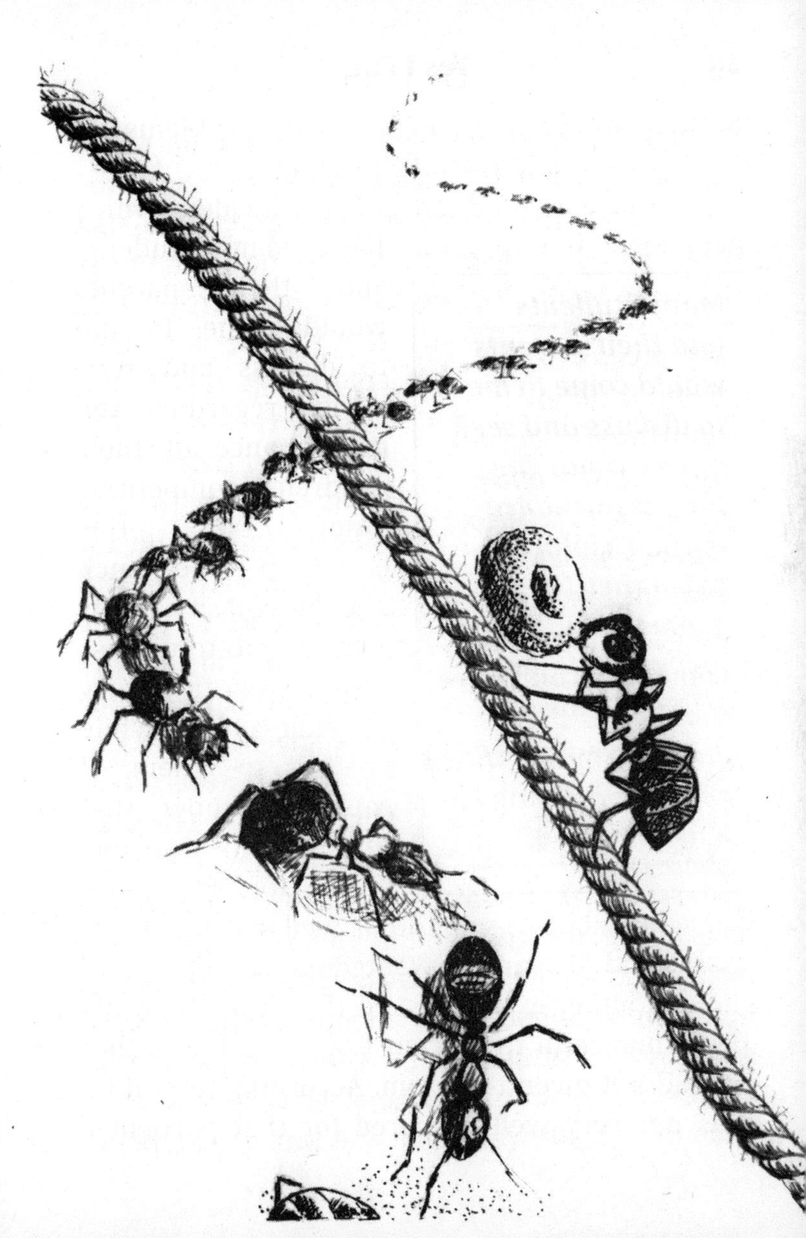

exam and would not be able to come up to his own expectations. I was surprised to hear the excuse and tried to make him understand that there would be many students, who would have the same feeling before the exam. I further told him that he is neither competing with the examiners nor with his teachers. He is only competing with his other fellow students who are also in the same boat. I further told him that I was sure that, if he would have given the exam, he would have done fairly well. I tried to make him further understand that sometimes in life you need to have a default answer for yourself, when you face an opportunity. What is an exam? Exam is not a punishment. It is an opportunity and a gateway to a future where you will explore new and exciting things. So whenever you know that you are at a gateway in life, the way you respond

What is an exam? Exam is not a punishment. It is an opportunity and a gateway to a future where you will explore new and exciting things. So whenever you know that you are at a gateway in life, the way you respond to it, is the key.

to it, is the key. What happens with many people is that they over think just the way this student did. He thought he might not be well prepared for that particular exam. And when I looked at his academic performance, I found that he was one of the best students in the school. He was doing everything up to the mark and then suddenly on the verge of the opportunity, he decided not to give the exam as he felt that he was not well prepared. This is what happens sometimes at the verge of the battle, you give up.

I tried to make him understand by citing an example of how the king Amir Timur learns a lesson from an ant. The king was distraught and lost a battle to his enemies. Humbled on the battlefield, the once mighty king retreated into the forest and took refuge in a cave.

I tried to make him understand by citing an example of how the king Amir Timur learns a lesson from an ant. The king was distraught and lost a battle to his enemies. Humbled on the battlefield, the once mighty king retreated into the forest and took refuge in a cave. As he rested against a hard rock in the damp cold of the forest cave, the king noticed a little black ant as it struggled to carry a grain up a slope on a wall. The wall was wet and slippery and the first attempt of the ant was a failure. The grain slipped from its hold and fell on the ground.

Undaunted, the ant retraced its steps, picked up the grain and started again on the arduous journey up the slippery wall. This time the ant negotiated a little distance. The grain slipped and fell once more.

Undaunted, the ant retraced its steps, picked up the grain and started again on the arduous journey up the slippery wall. This time the ant negotiated a little distance. The grain slipped and fell once more. The process repeated itself seven times. Each time, the ant started its uphill task afresh, not discouraged by the failures of the past. The seventh time, it found its footing and successfully carried the grain on to its destination. The king was inspired by the efforts of this little ant. "What is this ant trying to teach me?", he asked himself. "If a little ant can labour so hard to carry a single grain to its destination, surely I can struggle with determination to regain my throne." He marched forth, and in a pitched battle defeated his enemies and reclaimed his throne.

So let me now help you by introspecting. My default answer for an opportunity is Yes. For example, suppose somebody sends me a message and says this is a project that he wants to build with me. My first answer always would be yes. I would try to evaluate it to the best of my ability and as you know I would try to get it done somehow. But on the other hand, if I really feel it doesn't work, then I might leave it there and then. As my default answer to an opportunity is yes, it helps me to cut down my thinking process. My default answer at his stage would be to enable me to use all the possible available gateways which means I would

My default answer for an opportunity is Yes. For example, suppose somebody sends me a message and says this is a project that he wants to build with me. My first answer always would be yes. I would try to evaluate it to the best of my ability and as you know I would try to get it done somehow.

appear in all the exams that I'm eligible for and then see later. I would never over think before the gateway, "I would never want to be in position in later life where I am regretting the chances that I didn't take."

While he was speaking, my own mind was recollecting of so many of opportunities that I had said no to in my career, as I was afraid that I would mess up. I had also seen many a times, my colleagues less talented than me, taking up the challenges and be successful. Who knows if I would have taken those challenges, life would have been different. Might be somewhere while growing up my default answer changed from an emphatic Yes to a whimpering not-sure. Might be I needed to see my teacher once again and his motivating words and positive attitude would fill me with courage to say Yes to the challenges in life.

All we need sometimes is a default 'Yes' response.

He waved good bye to me. And before I could say anything, he said: see you tomorrow.

□

3

Power of Optimism

On the next day evening, I was waiting for him in his study room and thinking about myself for doing more and achieving more. I could understand what sir had told me about having positive attitude and the power of saying Yes. But a part of me was little sceptical about it also. What if I fail? Would I become a joke in front of my colleagues? So I decided to raise my questions to him to clear my doubts rather than a silent listener to his lecture and would try to open up to today's conversation with him. And then I saw him entering the room and felt that he was a person for whom age has had very little effect—same energy, same radiance as years before I met him. We started our daily ritual of greeting each other. Then I asked him about my becoming unusually cynical and pessimistic. He looked at me as if he was expecting it about me being so pessimistic and looked into my eyes for a moment. Then, he started speaking making sure that I understand each of his line.

It seems like we are all drowned in an ocean of negativity. This entire scenario is actually very scary. Let me give you the other side of this approach, which will help you to sail through this and would help you to understand the required perspective.

"When you switch on the TV today, you get scared to see that there is a pandemic of negativity all around. You switch on the Internet. You find the social media thriving on the negativity. It seems like we are all drowned in an ocean of negativity. This entire scenario is actually very scary. Let me give you the other side of this approach, which will help you to sail through this and would help you to understand the required perspective. I believe that there is a force that is innate to being human, a force which is probably behind the entire human creativity: The force of optimism.

Now tell me—What do you think is the

Half Empty

difference between a human and animal? I feel animals live only to defend themselves, have food and mate. They don't seek or believe in any other purpose of life. But we humans have ability of complex reasoning, our use of complex language, our ability to solve difficult problems and introspection. We also have the ability for creativity or the feeling of joy or sorrow is unique. Humans have a highly developed brain that allows us to do many of these things. There are two kinds of humans or may be three kinds of people. The one who will look at the glass and say the glass is half empty and he would not value what is inside. This one is a pessimist. Second is the optimist that will look at the glass and say the glass is half full. Let's make use of what is in the glass rather than worrying about what is not there. And the third is the one who will say this glass is totally full. This third type of people are visionaries because they know even when the glass is half empty, it has air inside. So it has air and water. It is actually full and these are the people, who know there is a value to everything. I want you to be that visionary right now. Be so strong that nothing can disturb your peace of mind. Look at the sunny side of everything.

As you know that very hard truth of life is that neither the good times nor the bad times last. But we want good times to last forever, but they don't. In a same way bad times also don't last forever and we should be thankful for it. You have to believe that the hard times will pass. There will be a world again full of bigger dreams, higher purpose for bigger ideas. As everything would come back to the normal one day. Are you ready? Are you ready to take advantage of that? Optimistic people tend to place their bet in believing that one day the world will be better and they put more efforts because they are more optimistic about the results. So what is required right now is optimism, massive optimism. Let's start looking at things with a more positive manner, start looking at everything that you have. Think only of the best, work only for the best, and expect only the best.

You have to believe that the hard times will pass. There will be a world again full of bigger dreams, higher purpose for bigger ideas. As everything would come back to the normal one day.

Forget the mistakes of the past and plan for

greater achievements of the future.

According to Benjamin Franklin: If you want to be optimistic learn the phrase, 'do it now' and stop the habit of procrastination. The saddest words in life are:

- 'It might have been'.
- 'I should have'.
- 'I could have'.
- 'I wish I had'.
- 'If only I had given a little extra'.

'Never leave till tomorrow which you can do today'.

—Benjamin Franklin

The question now is not what you don't have. The question is what do you have and how can you make the best use of the resources you have.

Count your blessings, not your troubles. Take time to smell the roses. We are so focused on complaining about things we don't have, that we lose sight of the things we have. There is a lot to be thankful for. Many of our blessings are hidden treasures–count your blessings and not your troubles.

The humans as a race have to survive every

calamity or disaster so far. We would be able to come out of this pandemic as well. If we are able to come out of this, then there will be opportunities, options, dreams coming true again. So, am I well prepared for that? So you should replace the negative thoughts and emotions with positive intent and hope. It will require some self resolution on your part to stay positive and if you are able to create that positivity and energy of optimism inside you, you will become a force and that force will help you to take things forward, create rhythm, momentum, break barriers and achieve your dreams.

It will require some self resolution on your part to stay positive and if you are able to create that positivity and energy of optimism inside you, you will become a force and that force will help you to take things forward, create rhythm, momentum, break barriers and achieve your dreams.

His words sounded like energy to me; they were entering my soul not the ears. Words were hitting the heart without bothering my mind. I felt recharged. May be I was concentrating on negativity too much, which was stopping my progress. I have to get away from the past. Dust myself off, get back into the mainstream. Put my dreams together and move forward. Thinking of the positive things that are true, honest and good, will put me in a positive state of mind.

If we want to build and maintain a positive attitude, we need to consciously practice the following steps:

I need to follow my heart with faith and enthusiasm. Yes the glass is full. I will come tomorrow to meet him again. Even if he doesn't invite me, I need to hear more from my Teacher.

□

4

Stop Comparing, Start Living

While waiting for him today, I started scrolling through my social media feed and came to know that one of my colleagues had bought a new car and another friend of mine had posted few photographs of his from Canada where he recently shifted for a new job. Going all through this, I started feeling very low with inferiority complex. I got really very restless. And when, Sir came, I asked him straightaway, didn't you ever feel that you could have done better in life. You are just a school teacher and you might be having friends and colleagues who are administrators, leaders and better placed in life than you. Didn't you ever feel inadequate and unhappy.

He looked at me with a very strange gaze and said first of all you should stop comparing yourself to others. Yet, that's often easier said than done. Job title, income, grades, house—the number of categories, in which we can compare ourselves to others are infinite. So is the number of people one can compare ourselves to.

> ***He looked at me with a very strange gaze and said first of all you should stop comparing yourself to others.... Comparison is generally the fast track to unhappiness. It's a recipe for misery. All it does is keeping you focused on what you don't like about yourself and your life.***

Comparison is generally the fast track to unhappiness. It's a recipe for misery. All it does is keeping you focused on what you don't like about yourself and your life. Recently, a friend of mine told me that he bought a Honda car. He was very, very happy and excited about it. He felt that he has upgraded himself by buying a bigger car. He wanted to share his happiness with one of his very close friends. He went to his friend's place and to his surprise found out that his friend had a bigger car, Audi. And immediately he lost all his enthusiasm, happiness and excitement. So when we focus on other

DON'T COMPARE
YOURSELF TO OTHERS.
EVERYONE HAS THEIR
OWN ROLE TO PLAY.

people, we lose time that we could otherwise invest in ourselves. We don't grow green grass by focusing on our neighbour's garden, we do it nurturing our own. So, instead of wasting time comparing your path to someone else's, spend it investing, creating, and caring for your own.

We tend to focus on their success. Instead of letting other people's triumphs get you down, let them open up possibilities for you. Let them be inspiration for what you can be, do and have in life.

Instead of resisting or fighting where you are, come to peace with it. Say yes to every part of your life, and from that place, make decisions that will move you in the right direction. There will always be someone who's richer, smarter, and more attractive than you. We tend to compare our behind-the-scenes with someone else's big moment. We tend to focus on their success. Instead of letting other people's triumphs get you down, let them open up possibilities for you. Let them be inspiration for what you can be, do and have in life. We often say things such as, "I should have this by now" or "I should have come further." But statements like that just keep us focused on what we're lacking. Instead of using 'should' when expressing commitments, use 'want' and notice how your inner dialogue shifts.

Our benchmark for success in life should be based on a meter, which is placed inside us. It should not be based on what others are doing. We can always choose to see. Imagine if instead of looking at a friend who was having a car, which is bigger than him, if he could have looked at scores of people, who don't even have a bicycle, he would have been more happy, more grateful about things. So far what I've learned in life is that the biggest poison in this world is, thinking about what other people are doing and what they are saying and what they want you to do. You become a sort of puppet to others and these people are least bothered about you. But you are somehow losing your happiness because pleasure of that comparison.

If somebody comes to me and tells me that my competitor is doing this or pursuing that, I don't care. I am leading my own life. I am just concerned about the goal of my life which is to be a better person, to improve my teaching skills, touch more lives and to do better than what I was doing yesterday. My competition is only with me. I would like to tell you that If you need to compare yourself with someone, compare yourself with you. What can you do to improve your life quality? How can you be a better and more loving person? How can you be nicer to yourself than you were yesterday? You are the only person you can compare yourself with.

> ***My competition is only with me. I would like to tell you that If you need to compare yourself with someone, compare yourself with you. What can you do to improve your life quality? How can you be a better and more loving person? How can you be nicer to yourself than you were yesterday?***

And, you know, what would I get by looking at competition all the time? Like I said, it's usually an unfair comparison to start with. As a result, I will always come off bad if l look at someone's strengths (including what they have, like houses and cars) and my weaknesses. Even if I compare strength to strength, there will always be those who are better, and those who are worse. Where we are on the ladder of accomplishments or purchases has nothing to do with what we want to do.

Problem of today is that children of your age group sometimes get so engaged and focused on what their friends are doing. When you look at somebody putting up a happy picture on Instagram, doesn't that really mean their life is much more exciting and happier than yours. We cannot compare to people putting up their choicest, their selected happiest or probably the most exciting moments. You are comparing your truth with their projected life.

Problem of today is that children of your age group sometimes get so engaged and focused on what their friends are doing. When you look at somebody putting up a happy picture on Instagram, doesn't that really mean their life is much more exciting and happier than yours.

You recently bought a Honda car but you want to show off to your friend who has bought a bigger car than yours. Imagine, you take a loan and you buy a car that you don't need. You put your money that you could have put into a business or use it for your son's education or you could have done something more worthwhile. You put that money into buying another car with a bank loan. And, then, you work overtime day and night. You spoil your life just to pay for the car that you want to show off to the man who really doesn't care about what car you drive.

> ***You know, you need to find your happiness. You have one life and you deserve to be happy. Count your blessings. A better focus is on what you do have and what you are already blessed with. Count what you have, not what you don't.***

When we keep comparing ourselves with others, we give them infinite power over our behaviour. We start subconsciously or unconsciously trying to follow or appease people.

I do not compare myself to anybody because I believe each individual has his/her own story to tell in this world. Each individual has his own journey. My journey might not be as exciting as yours, but it is mine at the end of the day. And I value my journey. And second thing is, let's not work to please people. You know, you need to find your happiness. You have one life and you deserve to be happy. Count your blessings. A better focus is on what you do have and what you are already blessed with. Count what you have, not what you don't. Think about how lucky you are to have what you have, to have the people in your life who care about you, to be alive at all. Focus on your strengths. Instead of looking at your weaknesses, ask yourself what your strengths are. Celebrate them! Be proud of them. Don't brag, but feel good about them and work on using them to your best advantage. Be ok with imperfection. No one is perfect—intellectually, we all know that, but emotionally we seem to feel bad when we don't reach perfection. You aren't perfect and you never will be. I certainly am not, and I've learned to be ok with that. Sure, keep trying to improve, but don't think you'll ever be the 'perfect person'. If you look at it in a different way, that imperfection is what makes you who you are, you already are perfect.

You need to strive to be better than your own self from the past, but not with others. You need to know that you are a fighter. You need to win. You are on your own personal agenda. Focus on the journey. Don't focus on how you rank in comparison to others—life is not a competition. It's a journey. We are all on a journey, to find something, to become something, to learn, to create. That journey has nothing to do with how well other people are doing, or what they have. It has everything to do with what we want to do, and where we want to go. That's all you need to worry about. So you should concentrate on your own journey to create your own personal legend. You cannot let people's opinion affect you. Competition is good in life. But comparison is not. You are on your own unique trajectory. You are God's creation. You have a purpose in life, which will be revealed to you in due course of time. Please have patience and continue being a better self than you were yesterday. Truly, there are no right or wrong in

That journey has nothing to do with how well other people are doing, or what they have. It has everything to do with what we want to do, and where we want to go. That's all you need to worry about. So you should concentrate on your own journey to create your own personal legend.

life and there is no absoluteness about correct approach to life. Let's not kill our individuality. Let's not kill our dreams and our goals in life just because we want to look like somebody else. Most people spend the majority of their time trying to please people they don't like and those people don't like them either, so it's just a mutual waste of time happening.

Instead, learn to realise that what you have is already enough. If you have shelter over your head, food on the table, clothes on your back, and people who love you, you are blessed. You have enough. Anything you have over and above that is more than enough. Be good with that, and you'll find contentment.

I know I have been hard hitting today, but I believe as a mentor, it's my duty to give you the correct perspective. You are unique. You are an asset to the world.

You are a unique individual with a unique journey creating a unique story on the sand of time. So to end this discussion I would say that learn to love enough. If you always want what others have, you will never have enough. You will always want more. That's an endless cycle, and it will never lead to happiness. No matter how many clothes you buy, no matter how many houses you own, no matter how many fancy cars you acquire...you'll never have enough. Instead, learn to realise that what you have is already enough. If you have shelter over your head, food on the table, clothes on your back, and people who love you, you are blessed. You have enough. Anything you have over and above that is more than enough. Be good with that, and you'll find contentment.

His words echoed in my mind on that day and till today whenever I find myself trapped in this endless game of comparison, I recall his words and feel the hand of my mentor stopping me from falling into this trap of comparison. I am unique. And my story will be legendary.

□

5

Finding your 'Mojo' Back

Today I was wondering about what my SS Sir had explained to me so far. All of what he said was not anything new to me, rather these were almost my own thoughts in my subconscious mind. All of this I had known all along but I lost my way somewhere on the way. Where has my mojo i.e. my confidence, passion, zeal, energy and enthusiasm for doing things, gone? Why I have changed as a person? What should I do to get my spirit, my mojo back?

Sir looked at my and replied:

"I want to take you way back to when you were in class sixth or seventh. Do you remember those days, when the teacher in the class would ask you, what would you like to become in life? And many of you would stand up and say, doctor, engineer, judge, administrator or a policeman etc.

It appeared as if you all have a compass inside you, which was showing the way to all of you. It was pulling you, making you work harder. As a result many of you were able to push yourself to the limits so that you could walk into an exciting future. Every year I meet a number of students who come back to me and say, Sir, why I was a different kind of student when I was in school and today I don't identify myself with my own old self. Inspiration, Get up and go, Motivation, Zest for life are no longer there. Losing this makes me feel uninspired and quite frankly, I don't feel like to act. I have become so lethargic and directionless. I have become somebody who I never was. I somehow lost my mojo, confidence and my spirit. I'm neither curious nor excited any longer about any new thing.

> ***I don't identify myself with my own old self. Inspiration, Get up and go, Motivation, Zest for life are no longer there. Losing this makes me feel uninspired and quite frankly, I don't feel like to act. I have become so lethargic and directionless.***

Sir further continued, I know many students

TEACHER
ARTIST
ARCHITECT
DOCTOR
SINGER
FARMER
DESIGNER
PILOT
SOLDIER
DENTIST
ENGENEER
NURSE
SCIENTIST

who got into the field of medicine, engineering and worked hard for four to five years to become doctors or engineers. And once they get there, they feel as if they have won the game. While in reality, they have just entered into a big field which further requires good hard work to get them established.

Trust me, no profession is simple, whether it is medicine, law, computer science, or art. In school, you just had an impression of the field but you had no idea about the depth of the subject. To become the master of any field you need to explore the subject deeply which requires a lot of hard work. There is a lot more to learn than you realise.

Now let's come back to the question about what was the difference between you of your school time and today? Answer is when you were in school, you had this compass pointing towards your dream, you didn't look around and did not debate too much about ifs and buts.

But there are some children who are identified by their teachers as highly intelligent. They compared how subjects fared throughout childhood and into adulthood; and that the most successful in life had key characteristics, including perseverance and willpower. These characteristics tend to be part of an individual's overall personality, but they are also something you can improve. Learning to persist in the face of challenges, and waiting for the rewards of your hard work can often be the key to success in life. Research by psychologist Carol Dweck suggests that there are two basic mindsets that influence how people think about themselves and their abilities: the fixed mindset and the growth mindset. People who possess a fixed mindset believe that things such as intelligence are static and unchangeable. Those with a fixed mindset believe that success isn't a result of hard work—it's simply a consequence of innate talents. Because

They compared how subjects fared throughout childhood and into adulthood; and that the most successful in life had key characteristics, including perseverance and willpower. These characteristics tend to be part of an individual's overall personality, but they are also something you can improve.

they believe that such talents are something people are either born with or without, they tend to give up more easily in the face of a challenge and loose their mojo. They quit when things do not come easily because they believe that they lack the inborn skill needed to excel. On the other hand, those who have a growth mindset, feel that they can change, grow, and learn through effort. People who believe that they are capable of growth are more likely to achieve success. When things get tough, they look for ways to improve their skills and keep working toward success.

> ***They tend to give up more easily in the face of a challenge and loose their mojo.... Those who have a growth mindset, feel that they can change, grow, and learn through effort. People who believe that they are capable of growth are more likely to achieve success.***

Now I will tell you normally what happens is that many people will be happy till the time they get their first success. You were happy about everything you were studying. You were not bothered about too many things you had to study and you had no baggage. But when you have your first success in your bag, you need to hold on to your success and you become slightly insecure about it and then you need to work on it. But some times you consult wrong people and then you end up in mess and get more insecure about it. In this vicious circle of insecurity. you become a totally different person. Then, inevitably, you hit a plateau. Stagnation sets in and you lose your mojo which refers to desire, passion, or motivation. You're not the same person who was attacking life with great enthusiasm and suddenly you're more defensive. You lose that touch, that offence that made you win in the first place. You are afraid to go all out and you start feeling I'm not good enough. And you start feeling like an imposter who did well in school by chance and now you don't deserve to be in the position that you are.

But when you have your first success in your bag, you need to hold on to your success and you become slightly insecure about it and then you need to work on it.... Stagnation sets in and you lose your mojo which refers to desire, passion, or motivation.

Most important drive in life is having a purpose or goal. You'll see it, when you believe it. Envision your finish line and feel what it would take to attain your goal. Work backward to determine what it takes to reach that point. Setting small, incremental goals for each stage of the process will help keep you focussed and keep your mind alert. You'll see the manifested outcome of all that you believed. Every one of us has an invisible compass inside. Once you understand it, once you find it that this is where I am headed, you will be able to do better. You have to make your mark in the limited time that you have; you need to identify and find that compass inside you, just like you had in school, a

Every one of us has an invisible compass inside. Once you understand it, once you find it that this is where I am headed, you will be able to do better. You have to make your mark in the limited time that you have; you need to identify and find that compass inside you, just like you had in school, a compass pointing to a great career, a meaningful life.

compass pointing to a great career, a meaningful life. You need to get back to that compass every now and then to find your mojo back.

Here I was wondering how true it was; in school, offence was my way of life and I was not bothered about consequences. I only believed in my hard work and I truly believed that miracles are possible. It is true after landing a so called good job, I became insecure and I was working to hold on to the job rather than create value. I have to give my 100%, may be 110% to the game again. I have to be on the offence. I need to get back that spirit I had in school.

Getting your mojo back is critical for your quality of life for some radical changes and the outright shattering of your own conventional wisdom. Face it, feel passionate and motivated every day for your work, family and self. It will be a win for yourself and those who depend on you.

□

6

Moderately Successful Paradox

The next day I told Sir at least I have a Job, if I take a risk and what if I lose everything I have gained so far. Then where should I draw a line of dissatisfaction and unhappiness .

Sir replied: Please listen to me carefully today. Once you become moderately successful in life you try to cling on to the status quo. A moderately successful person has clear and limited targets and is happy when he accomplishes them. He is satisfied, settles with it and works hard to maintain it. What if in three years you become a cricketer who plays district level matches and then retires without playing international cricket at all? Or what if you become a man who was moderately doing well, but never top the game? Imagine you being an actor, who is always

getting, a cameo or a short role in the movies but could never actually make a mark. So that's a risk bigger than risk of trying. Where as a highly successful person is usually the one who is the best in his field or what he does. Tough to replace or compete with. He has a mission that gets him excited to wake up everyday. The passion for what he does, drives him crazy to work towards it continuously. There is no concept of settling as the goal is to be the best in what he does and this is a continuous effort. He is satisfied with challenges, progress, growth and the journey to be the best.

> ***Where as a highly successful person is usually the one who is the best in his field or what he does. Tough to replace or compete with. He has a mission that gets him excited to wake up everyday. The passion for what he does, drives him crazy to work towards it continuously.***

That's the fear you have. You always want to do more because you want to explore your limits, want to expand and face the challenges but you are scared of failure. So you don't try and get satisfied with what you have. Here I would like to tell you that there are two things which are very different but many people take them as synonyms: Happiness and Satisfaction. What makes an individual happy? What makes a person feel satisfied? Can someone be satisfied even if he's not happy, or will he find happiness even when he's not completely satisfied. Knowing the difference between happy and satisfied can be tricky. Throughout life, we strive for happiness while also having wants that need to be satisfied. But, how are they different and is it possible to be both happy and satisfied?

Can someone be satisfied even if he's not happy, or will he find happiness even when he's not completely satisfied. Knowing the difference between happy and satisfied can be tricky. Throughout life, we strive for happiness while also having wants that need to be satisfied.

Happiness and satisfaction are two very different states of mind. If you're satisfied with your life and your achievements, then you stop asking for more because you're satisfied with what you have. So we can say that satisfaction is a state of contentment where all of your desires have been met. You typically find it in possessions and the enjoyment of things that you desire. Meeting the desires of your heart, as well as the demands of your needs, doesn't mean that you'll necessarily be happy– despite the fact that you will never want for anything more when you are satisfied.

> ***Happiness and satisfaction are two very different states of mind. If you're satisfied with your life and your achievements, then you stop asking for more because you're satisfied with what you have.***

So then what is happiness?

Happiness is defined as both an emotion and state. It's a subjective term used to describe a wide-range of positive emotions, such as joy, pride, contentment, and gratitude. The experience of joy, contentment, or positive well-being, combined with a sense that one's life is good, meaningful, and worthwhile.

Happiness is the journey that we are in. Happiness is in exploring challenges. Happiness is expanding your abilities, your perspectives every day. I agree there will be differences in opinion, as it is a difficult topic that we are looking at today.

For example, to me, a great artist creates to make somebody feel something deep or unexpected. Anyone can make art, but not everyone can make you feel something when viewing their art. Most artists don't create because they want to, they create because they have to. There is a force calling on them to create more and want to improve. Good artists turn that energy into something beautiful. They use it to fuel their creativity and make work that resonates with others.

Entrepreneurship demands having initiative and a strong determination to succeed. It also requires an immense amount of confidence, tenacity and independence.

Similarly when I look at all the successful entrepreneurs, I find that they're the most unhappy people with what they've achieved so far. Entrepreneurship demands having initiative and a strong determination to succeed. It also requires an immense amount of confidence, tenacity and independence. They always want to do more and improve; and I feel that this slight amount of dissatisfaction in life creates the hunger to do more, to create more, to improvise. And what we see in the world today is a result of a human being's dissatisfaction with the status quo. We were not happy with the horses. We never wanted to sit on a horse chariot any longer. We improvised. We discovered and made motorcycles & motor cars. It's all a result of not being satisfied with the status quo and always wanting to improve and discover new things.

Happiness is not an achievement but a state. Happiness is in trying to be a better self and to explore new things, identifying your hidden talents, expanding your abilities, stretching your limits etc.

The original topic that I want to discuss today with you is a phenomenon called as moderately successful. As a person, I don't want myself to be moderately successful and as a mentor I don't want you also to be moderately successful. I may not be the best, but I would always strive for more. I don't want to be an average. I don't want to be an actor who lived his entire life doing supporting roles. So you have to seek more. What if you were a cricketer that nobody knew? What if you become a player that nobody bothered about? Happiness comes from challenging ourselves. It's when we're engaged, stimulated, and discovering. It comes from tackling the next assignment in our life, and from working toward the next mountain, and then the next. That next is somewhere you have to seek more leaving a legacy, making a mark, creating a story worth telling and then making an episode of that story every day. Don't be satisfied with the status quo. Push harder; push to make a dent in the universe.

To be greedy means to seek what is not yours. I'm not talking about being greedy. I'm talking about being dissatisfied with the status quo and long to improve, to do better, pursue new journey, create a legacy, leave a mark and feel happy in what you're doing.

I further would like to tell you that don't confuse happiness with greed. I keep getting a lot of messages from my students saying, don't you think Sir that always striving for more is not being greedy. To be greedy means to seek what is not yours. I'm not talking about being greedy. I'm talking about being dissatisfied with the status quo and long to improve, to do better, pursue new journey, create a legacy, leave a mark and feel happy in what you're doing. Don't be satisfied for moderate success always, try to thrive for higher goals and face new challenges every day with full zeal and zest.

"*You may win. You may lose. That's different. But always dream for bigger achievements.*"

As the discussion ended, I knew what was wrong in my life, I was getting comfortable with my moderate success and was clinging on to it. I was on a defensive mode rather than challenging myself. But now I need to seek more. I want to make a dent in the universe. I want to leave a legacy.

□

7

Message to Younger self

I was getting myself prepared to go back to the city and join my office. Suddenly I heard some noises from the next room. Everyone in the family was glued to the television. There was some news about lockdown being extended and interstate travel was also blocked. Here I got stuck once again in my home town and then suddenly I realised that it all just got too much for me. I sat at my work desk on the brink of tears, frustration and disappointment and I started feeling a void for not being able to join my office, meeting friends and follow my routine. The feelings of grief and loneliness made me angry also. I controlled myself and started thinking how to overcome this thought and spend this further extended lockdown time.

However then I remembered about my last few days spent with my favourite teacher and felt a surge of gratitude. Suddenly this divine signal became my inner desire to spend some more time with him. This gave me a sense of purpose and brought me joy and comfort and made me to believe that I could navigate my life because our future is mapped out.

> ***However then I remembered about my last few days spent with my favourite teacher and felt a surge of gratitude. Suddenly this divine signal became my inner desire to spend some more time with him.***

I was pulled to his residence. There I found him sitting in his lawn having a cup of tea. He looked at me and smiled as if he was expecting me. He offered me also a cup of tea. He was in a very happy mood today. Looking at his face, I wondered whether a man like him ever had any regrets in his life. If given a chance what would he want to tell his younger self. I questioned this to him.

He started replying:

We all normally try to seek advice from other people. But we forget that the most important person from whom we can get advice is our inner self.

YOU CAN'T DO IT
YOU DON'T HAVE
A
CHANCE
IMPOSSIBLE

The foremost thing that I would like to tell my younger self and would like to tell you as well, is that nothing is impossible in this world; it is just an opinion by other people. So don't listen to them. From the time we begin to believe in ourselves, people begin to tear our confidence down. They tell us things like, "You can't do that!", "That's not possible!", "You can't change that!", "Don't waste your time!", "You are making a big mistake!", "You don't have a chance!" Just as we let our parents convince us that we can do anything, we begin to let others convince us that we can't. Just as we accept that we can be whoever we want to be and allow others to persuade us that we will never be more than we are now. Sooner or later you will realise that whatever you think is impossible but

The foremost thing that I would like to tell my younger self and would like to tell you as well, is that nothing is impossible in this world; it is just an opinion by other people. So don't listen to them. From the time we begin to believe in ourselves, people begin to tear our confidence down.

there would be somebody else who would make it possible. Always remember that impossible is just a word thrown around by trivial men who find it easier to live in the world they've been given than to explore the power they have to change it. Impossible is not a fact. It's an opinion, temporary and nothing.

That success comes to you if you relentlessly come back to your cause or aim in life. I have always been thinking, what makes somebody successful and what works in their favour.

The next thing that I thought I would want my younger self to know that success comes to you if you relentlessly come back to your cause or aim in life. I have always been thinking, what makes somebody successful and what works in their favour. Over the years, I realised that people who are successful by the worldly definition of success are people who set their goals and also commit to achieve them so to maximise the likelihood of success and also have an 'I must do this' attitude. When you don't have this, you risk putting off what you need to do to make the goal a reality. This is not you.

Now I would like to tell you what do I mean by coming back to your cause? Right from the childhood, you start developing a compass inside you. This compass is pointing towards your destined pathway which you really want to follow in your life. It is pointing towards doing what would make you feel happy. The key here is that, as you know that we all have a compass pointing towards our destined pathway but sometimes when you have magnetic fields disturbing a compass, the needle will sway. You get distracted in the path in many ways. Sometime you meet people who tell you that whatever you have been thinking or doing is wrong and what you are chasing is impossible. If you believe them, you realise that you have done a blunder and a feeling of insecurity comes. As you grow, you would acquire a burden of mistakes you

> ***As you grow, you would acquire a burden of mistakes you have made. The difference is the people who do well in life are able to take failures as a stepping stone to the next success. They try to learn from it. They don't believe that it is a failure.***

have made. The difference is the people who do well in life are able to take failures as a stepping stone to the next success. They try to learn from it. They don't believe that it is a failure. They believe it's a learning experience.

That statistic may make you uneasy, but it's one worth knowing. Failing once, twice, or even hundred of times doesn't mean you've hit the end of the road–it means you've taken another turn, and you're one step closer to success.

People see success as positive and failure as negative. You can learn, grow and evolve from your past mistakes. That statistic may make you uneasy, but it's one worth knowing. Failing once, twice, or even hundred of times doesn't mean you've hit the end of the road–it means you've taken another turn, and you're one step closer to success. As you go through the life and encounter failures, you'll learn valuable life lessons from the mistakes done.

The goal today is to help you learn from your failures and become more successful and productive. It's often said that failure doesn't stop people, it's how people handle failure that stops them. When you encounter failure, tackle it head on and learn from your mistakes. Realise that every idea that pops up in your mind isn't going to work. Take the time to organise your thoughts after a failure and realise what you did wrong. Above all else, be willing to learn and grow.

When you encounter failure, tackle it head on and learn from your mistakes. Realise that every idea that pops up in your mind isn't going to work. Take the time to organise your thoughts after a failure and realise what you did wrong. Above all else, be willing to learn and grow.

Further I want to explain to you regarding the feeling of insecurity in you. We are all blessed that we are born as humans. We have immense potential and ability. But when you become insecure, you suddenly open up yourself to various opinions of different people who are in touch with you. In normal course of time, you are not bothered about their opinions. But when you have a feeling of insecurity, you open a window to let people question your ability. One of the primary reasons that people question you regarding your ability is because you lack the right or proper motivation. So you amplify it, and you start believing that you are a failure and you would not be able to achieve your goals.

I would like to tell you today, the difference between people who are successful in their life and people who don't do well in life. Successful people relentlessly come back to their targets in life. They believe in themselves and the quote 'nothing is impossible'. They have a dream and have an aim as they know that without an aim they cannot achieve. To make their dream come true they must have faith in themselves. They come back to their target and internal compass, which is pointing to the way they want to lead their life. They don't go away just because people are saying it is impossible. The only limit to the height

They believe in themselves and the quote 'nothing is impossible'. They have a dream and have an aim as they know that without an aim they cannot achieve. To make their dream come true they must have faith in themselves.

of their achievements is the reach of their dreams and their willingness to work for them. Setting goals is the first step in turning the invisible into visible. If you have built castles in the air, your work need not be lost; you need to put the foundations under them. You should also know that goal is not always meant to be reached; it often serves simply as something to aim at.

> ***Sometimes things happen which are beyond your control. For example, as you know we are in the middle of a pandemic right now which we have never anticipated. We cannot do anything about it.***

Sometimes things happen which are beyond your control. For example, as you know we are in the middle of a pandemic right now which we have never anticipated. We cannot do anything about it. For people who do well in life believe dreams never hurt anybody if you keep working tirelessly to achieve the dream and make it a reality. No doubt you may encounter many defeats, In fact, it may be necessary sometimes to encounter the defeats to know who you are, what you can rise from, how you can still come out of it.

So they come back, and that too relentlessly.

It doesn't really matter what people are telling you, it doesn't really matter what is happening in the world. If you keep coming back to what you really want to do, you would make it big and this gives to your life all the confidence you need to do anything you want to do. Nothing is impossible for you. You have repeatedly proven that you can handle anything and overcome all the obstacles till this point in your life. If you don't remember anything else, remember this: the confidence that allowed you to mature as a child, is the same confidence that will allow you to be successful as an adult.

It doesn't really matter what people are telling you, it doesn't really matter what is happening in the world. If you keep coming back to what you really want to do, you would make it big and this gives to your life all the confidence you need to do anything you want to do.

Here I would like to mention a movie which I really like watching repeatedly. It is Rocky by Sylvester Stallone. I'm sure you must also have watched it. In this, the hero gets beaten black and blue by the opponent. But, if you notice, he always gets up at the end of every round; it is not about how hard you can hit the opponent rather it is about how hard you can be hit and then you still come back. I really feel that line in my soul.

□

8

Detached but Passionate

Next evening as I was going to meet my Sir, I was just thinking why my mind splits into two halves. One half of mine wanted to follow all that my teacher has taught me. Other half was sceptical. This other half wants guarantee for results. Even if I am not very happy in life, still I feel safe and satisfied with my present job as well with my life. In my pursuit for happiness and success by facing new challenges, I feel very insecure of losing everything. Before facing new challenges, I want to know about the result. If somehow, the results were guaranteed, I want to win but...

To clear my doubts SS Sir started telling me:

I had also been into same situations in my life where I felt anxious about what I'm doing and at the same time I had been in zones where

I was over concerned about the outcomes. If I remain solely motivated by the outcomes or consequences, I suffer from performance anxiety while in action. I feel demotivated if the expected results do not occur and I assume arrogance if the consequences do occur. So how did I manage this anxiety. I would like to share this with you in my own way of life.

> ***I had been in zones where I was over concerned about the outcomes. If I remain solely motivated by the outcomes or consequences, I suffer from performance anxiety while in action.***

Rule number one that I follow is what I term as detached passion. I know it sounds ambiguous but this is something I truly believe in, I truly practice it. Detached passion is the most potent pair of paradox in our life's journey. As we passionately engage in various activities, we usually get significantly attached to the results and that's what leads to increased stress in our life. Alternately, if we take a detached or a disinterested approach, it's not particularly supportive of our moving forward.

So you can say that the passion is for the task

at hand. The detachment is for the consequences of the action. Without passion, my actions will not have the emotional fuel to ignite. I will lose the opportunity to the possibility of a grand impact. This does not reflect on my actions. It does not lead to disappointment and consequently to my stopping the flapping of my wings. Hence, I try to detach myself from the consequences whenever I do something. Detachment saves you from anxiety, demotivation and arrogance. Following this principle of not getting emotional about the cause or intensely passionate about the work. I always tend to put my passion, my energy, my madness onto the task that I am doing. I like what I am doing. I enjoy what I am doing, and I don't take too much stress about the outcome. I keep telling myself that there

> ***Without passion, my actions will not have the emotional fuel to ignite. I will lose the opportunity to the possibility of a grand impact. This does not reflect on my actions. It does not lead to disappointment and consequently to my stopping the flapping of my wings.***

are only two repercussions possible. Either I will win or I will learn and I don't believe in winning or losing. This helps me taking my anxiety off because I am not looking it as the ultimate defeat. The anxiety happens when you think that this is my only attempt. This is the only opportunity I have.

Attachment to consequences robs us of passion to perform. Passionate detachment is not a contradiction in terms, it is a unified synergy that flows.

Detachment from consequences is not indifference to results. In fact, detachment helps me to dream big. Attachment to consequences leads to short-term, risk-free, controllable goals. Passion helps me focus on the here and now, leading to a sense of urgency. It helps me leverage my sense of mortality and transience, galvanising my energy

Attachment to consequences leads to short-term, risk-free, controllable goals. Passion helps me focus on the here and now, leading to a sense of urgency. It helps me leverage my sense of mortality and transience, galvanising my energy to the current window of opportunity.

to the current window of opportunity. It saves me from procrastination as tomorrow may not come for my life. Passion helps me act as if today is the last day of my life.

I want you to know that the world is full of opportunity today. Detach yourself from the consequences but be passionate about the cause. Imagine a student enjoying study, and then results would automatically come vs. someone who is overwhelmed by anxiety of the results. Think about focussing on the process, not the outcome. Talk about the effort that you have put in. Talk about the process. Look at entrepreneurs and high achievers. You will find this detachment from outcome in all high achievers. They do their best, but they don't punish themselves for a wrong outcome if they have done their best.

How often do we see students who mess up the first exam they give after a break. They get overwhelmed by the situation. They get very anxious. They lose decisiveness needed in the exam. How many times we see sportsmen losing the form after a break. Winning is a habit that needs to be cultivated. Students do it by giving mock exams, sportsmen do it by practise matches. They play and play till the time they start enjoying the process; and process is the part of their system. They learn the art of detached passion. You might say that you can't be detached and passionate at the same time. Detachment and passionate engagement are unlikely cousins as we often think of them as opposite ends of the spectrum, but what if they are at the same end, just different and equally important branches? What if detachment is needed so our identity does not become intertwined with our idea, our system, our technology, or the change we are seeking to bring about. But at the same time can we passionately engage listening, hearing, encouraging other perspectives and sharing our own so the change we desire comes to life? But when you see them in perspective of detachment from outcome, being passionate about the cause is the mantra of success. Passionate Detachment is useful and

Detachment and passionate engagement are unlikely cousins as we often think of them as opposite ends of the spectrum, but what if they are at the same end, just different and equally important branches?

reliable. Passionate Detachment works. Try it!

His words were echoing in my head and at the same time I was thinking of famous verse from *Bhagwadgita* which my teacher, my guru had explained to me so simply.

□

9

Being the Big man, Being the Eagle

Next few days, I couldn't meet my teacher. There were issues at home. My brother couldn't come back home from the city during the lockdown. This lockdown might have given me a perspective on slowing down as I spent more time with my family but it has also added to my responsibilities. The result is that a few months into lockdown, I was extremely feeling stressed out and anxious. However, coming to terms with loss of control over free movement and the resulting uncertainty was causing me to experience immense worry and anxiety. The social disconnect was also posing challenges, besides the additional workload at home. All this made me very furious and irritable. This entire pandemic had hit me financially also and I was feeling bitter about everything and everyone. Why should I be on the receiving end of things? Environment at the home with each passing day was getting worst. There was no news of opening up of the state borders. I got stuck also. As for to keep my morale high in these circumstances, I decided to meet my favourite Sir once again. He also looked happy to see me again. While seeing him, it appeared to me as if there had been no gap in our meetings. With all these meetings with him, now I always felt his eternal presence along. Looking at me, he asked about me being so tensed and stressful. I then told him about my feeling, being on the receiving end of all relationships!

The social disconnect was also posing challenges, besides the additional workload at home. All this made me very furious and irritable. This entire pandemic had hit me financially also and I was feeling bitter about everything and everyone.

Let me try to help you here and to make you feel relaxed, I would try my best to articulate my perspective.

When things are not going right in your job, in family, in your studies etc., the key is how you react in such circumstances and what kind of person you would become.

In every family when you look around today, you will find some member of the family act like a responsible person or you can say the leader. These are the people who have big heart to take the responsibility of everything or managing the show.

In every family when you look around today, you will find some member of the family act like a responsible person or you can say the leader. These are the people who have big heart to take the responsibility of everything or managing the show.

Imagine if you are handling a project along with another colleague of yours which is not going well. So how do you react to that?

Would you take the responsibility for all issues and obstacles that stand in the way of successful project delivery and would try to find out the solution of the problem, rather than stepping back. You would further plan and strategise the most effective ways to solve the problem and plan all the activities and resources needed to solve it. I know it's actually very difficult to do. But if you somehow are able to do this, you become a leader and trustworthy. And this is where, I ask you again now what is your default response when things go wrong?

It's very rosy when things go right, the only issue is who takes the credit; but when things go wrong, that is the real test of strength of character. And this strength of character must be consistent. Successful people are not going to give up that easily. If X went wrong, it does not affect Y which is the hallmark of their success. They are adaptable, resilient, and determined to go on. That means having a plan B ready so that the phoenix will rise from the ashes. I often feel in present scenario this is something which is lacking in today's culture. That is taking the responsibility of the failure.

That means having a plan B ready so that the phoenix will rise from the ashes. I often feel in present scenario this is something which is lacking in today's culture. That is taking the responsibility of the failure.

Rather you will find people are busy in finding faults. What about rising above the clouds? So here I would like to say that you must learn what type of a person you would like to become when things go wrong.

How do you rise as an individual? How do you rise above the clouds? There is a saying which talks about when there are rains and storms, the eagle rises above the clouds and flies. Are you an eagle or a man with a large heart who if fails, is prepared to move out of the safe comfort zone, able to sit down and assess calmly what went wrong, take calculated risks and hence experience the joy of growing and fulfilment. There is a lesson from every failure and you know how/where to find it, accept it, and above all apply it to future projects.

How do you rise as an individual? How do you rise above the clouds? There is a saying which talks about when there are rains and storms, the eagle rises above the clouds and flies.

Another thing which I always tell people is that secret of success is not in talent. There are so many people with talent not doing well; it happens with such regularity that people use this as a phrase 'wasted talent'.

You need to be a man of integrity, a man who knows how to rise above the clouds when things are down. How do you react? What is your default response? Could you just close your eyes today and analyse and compare your behaviour with your reaction in the last seven days when there was a difficult situation in the family or in your office front and now if you find yourself in the same situation? Would you be a big man or the leader who rises above the differences. Would you do that? I'm sure you will feel good, satisfied and relaxed.

> ***You need to be a man of integrity, a man who knows how to rise above the clouds when things are down. How do you react? What is your default response?***

We live in a competitive world because it is all about the survival of the fittest, the selfish wants, desires and demands of people who want more for less, the unending and unlimited wants and needs of people. No matter what world or industry you're in, it can be easy to think of your environment as cut-throat or competitive, especially if the pressure to succeed is constant and intense. Competing with and comparing yourself to others can set you up for jealousy, stress and exhaustion. The ultimate victory in competition is derived from the inner satisfaction of knowing that you have done your best and that you have got the most out of what you had. The success is not about how talented you are. Trust me, it is about the mindset, how the wiring in your brain is made to handle tough situations. You might ask me why should you handle tough situations? It is part of the game. Now do you understand—being a good student in school, you were easily winning. You never realised there would be a time where you will not be able to win and you will have to know how to react in this situation. Will you rise above your difficulties and stand tall and say, I will face it? Or you will be the one who will become a complaint box, start complaining about everybody and everything

Trust me, it is about the mindset, how the wiring in your brain is made to handle tough situations. You might ask me why should you handle tough situations? It is part of the game.

and become a cynical middle-age individual.

Don't forget—you are the captain of your own life. You need to rise above your past, ego, personality and aspirations. Do you rise above it to make the system run? That's when you will win and become the leader.

> ***You can become an eagle, who rises when there is rain or you can become a lizard, who hides when there is a problem. It's important to do your best and work hard, but it's equally important to remember that life is not all about competition.***

You can become an eagle, who rises when there is rain or you can become a lizard, who hides when there is a problem. It's important to do your best and work hard, but it's equally important to remember that life is not all about competition. Showing up to compete can yield business success but challenging yourself in healthy ways while feeling empowered can yield joy and happiness.

So when you face any problem in home front or in your job, always be the big man. You know, it's about being the big man.

I knew what Would I do once I reach home.

I very confidently told my family that I will try to solve all problems and issues even if it meant postponing my stay for few more days. It felt good and happy being the big man. I learnt the art of relationship from my teacher.

□

10

No Regrets

This year has been a whirlwind of ups and downs both personally and professionally. I think everyone has suffered some unforeseen setbacks but when I sit here and think about the past few months of my own life, I wouldn't have had it any other way.

I have always been considered as stubborn if not persistent in going after my goals. Everyone including myself suffers from moments when you think about your failures and sometimes moments of doubt which sometimes grow into moments of regret. I know that even the most successful persons have some failures and also suffer from some type of regret although possibly disguised as another emotion, it's almost impossible to not be affected.

So today I decided to ask Sir, which is more

painful—having failures or regrets.

Though l knew the answer but still I wanted to hear his words because his words always ignite my soul and motivate me.

His words of advice were:

To understand what we want to do in life, first of all we need to see people around and think what kind of person we would never like to become. To further explain this to you, have you ever visited any administrative office and seen how people work there and observed their working atmosphere. You will find some people looking blankly at the clock as if they are just waiting for five o'clock when their office time gets over.

To further explain this to you, have you ever visited any administrative office and seen how people work there and observed their working atmosphere. You will find some people looking blankly at the clock as if they are just waiting for five o'clock when their office time gets over.

Here I would like you to understand that this is what happens when you are doing something

Oops

which you really are not interested to do. You are doing it just for the sake of doing. So doing something without any interest results only in regret. It can never lead to learning or creating anything of value and therefore regret is debilitating and paralysing you. I would never like you to become a person who has accumulated many regrets or lived his life with regret of failures and fully aware of the outcome of his actions.

Time never matters when you do something of your interest and enjoy doing the same. Trust me, automatically the results, the output would become a lot more different and a lot more productive because you are not governed by time.

On the other hand doing something of your interest may result in failure but it gives you an opportunity to learn and improve from what you have experienced. So no time left to look at the clock blankly. Time never matters when you do something of your interest and enjoy doing the same. Trust me, automatically the results, the output would become a lot more different and a lot more productive because you are not governed by time. I want you to reach that zone where you start enjoying in what you are doing. The results automatically come. So one can say that having regrets means never exploring any means of achieving something and you keep looking at the time.

This is the biggest difference between the people who are in the high achievement zone and people who are not. It is all about—are you enjoying what you are doing and not becoming a clock gazer.

So in a nutshell, I would say that regret is a negative cognitive/emotional state where one feels sad or disappointed and involves blaming oneself for only bad outcome. With this feeling of regret, sometimes one would like to undo a choice previously made. Failure is an experience that teaches the way in which one could tackle the problems. It does not mean you have exhausted all avenues for exploration. You need to understand that there will be times when it is necessary to take two steps forward rather than take three steps backward. Failure is the string which ties every significant step in history. Could we have reached the moon without the brave sacrifice of those astronauts willing to risk their lives for the unknown? Could we have developed a vaccination against polio if Jonas Salk never tested it on himself? Significant learning only happens when it shares a bed with the opportunity for failure. Failure breeds understanding of the things that need to be fixed in order to achieve success. On the other hand regret is accepting what you are today and you will remain the same without any future progress.

Failure breeds understanding of the things that need to be fixed in order to achieve success. On the other hand regret is accepting what you are today and you will remain the same without any future progress.

While he was speaking, visuals of me working in my office and my frequent glances at the office clock were floating in my mind. I had become someone I never wanted to. I wanted to change. I wanted to live a wonderful and progressive life achieving all my goals. Yes, on my tombstone, I want to have the most important two words—NO REGRETS.

□

The Final Day

I hate Goodbye moments

As the city opens up after several months of lockdown and enters a new way of operation with safety as the focus, many people are still trying to grapple with the change. But I was very happy and thrilled as now I could go back to my work and my friends. The development of Covid-19 vaccine had delivered the promise of the miracle that we all hoped for. News channels were all cheerful and optimistic once again. I longed to go back to my work with new found enthusiasm. I decided to meet my teacher, my mentor last time with a promise to come back to him whenever I will visit my family. During my stay in lockdown period, I tried to solve lot of issues or problems my family was facing by being the responsible and big guy as advised by my favourite Sir. I also got myself ready for my future career plans with full enthusiasm and passion. I will try to do things that really matter to me and doing which I lose count of time. I promised to myself, that I will no longer be a clock gazer. I will never accumulate regrets of my life. I will try not to be moderately successful.

> ***I also got myself ready for my future career plans with full enthusiasm and passion. I will try to do things that really matter to me and doing which I lose count of time. I promised to myself, that I will no longer be a clock gazer. I will never accumulate regrets of my life. I will try not to be moderately successful.***

I wanted to give my teacher a parting gift. A gift of Gratitude. My soul got rekindled by a spark from his words. I also knew deep in my heart that the highest appreciation is not to utter words of thankfulness, but I would try to live as per the advice given to me by my mentor, my guide—SS Sir.

So, I got my ticket for 4:00 o'clock train and decided to stop by his residence on the way back to the station. When I reached his residence, I came to know that he has gone to meet his friend and will be back in the late evening. My time to catch the train was running short. I was feeling sad that I am not able to meet him and thank him for all his motivating words which changed me and my thinking process completely. At this point, I felt as if he knew about my going back and would not like to meet me as I no longer needed him. With passing days, he found me a completely changed person with positive attitude and enthusiasm. He knew that I no longer needed his wisdom and I am sure he also hated goodbyes like me. I closed my eyes and thanked him from the core of my heart. I believe that the hearts which are connected can talk through distance. I knew he wants me to carry the torch of winning to the next generation which would be my perfect act of gratitude to him.

With passing days, he found me a completely changed person with positive attitude and enthusiasm. He knew that I no longer needed his wisdom and I am sure he also hated goodbyes like me.

□

Epilogue

I left my school job and joined a local college as a Physics teacher. I wanted to make a difference and leave a legacy. I spent hours and hours after my teaching hours with my students. I like to teach them how to think rather than what to think. 30 years down the line, today I am retiring from my college. Many of my ex-students also came to meet me. Their words of gratitude made me feel worthwhile. I always wanted to live a full life. I always believe that the strength of a person's life is the stories he/she has left behind. Carve your name on hearts, not tombstones. I always remember my teacher; and hope I will always live in the hearts of my students with their recognition, respect and appreciation for me.

> *"Legacy is not leaving something for people. It's leaving something in people."*
>
> **—Peter Strople**

□□□